HAL•LEONARD
INSTRUMENTAL
PLAY-ALONG

AUDIO
ACCESS
INCLUDED

PLAYBACK+
Speed • Pitch • Balance • Loop

HORN

ADELE

T0070693

To access audio visit:
www.halleonard.com/mylibrary

Enter Code
1735-2711-9306-7721

ISBN 978-1-4950-6300-8

HAL•LEONARD®
CORPORATION
7777 W. BLUEMOUND RD. P.O. BOX 13819 MILWAUKEE, WI 53213

Visit Hal Leonard Online at
www.halleonard.com

ALL I ASK

Horn

Words and Music by ADELE ADKINS,
PHILIP LAWRENCE, BRUNO MARS
and CHRIS BROWN

CHASING PAVEMENTS

Horn

Words and Music by ADELE ADKINS
and FRANCIS EG WHITE

HELLO

Horn

Words and Music by ADELE ADKINS
and GREG KURSTIN

MAKE YOU FEEL MY LOVE

HORN

Words and Music by
BOB DYLAN

MILLION YEARS AGO

Horn

Words and Music by ADELE ADKINS
and GREGORY KURSTIN

REMEDY

Horn

Words and Music by ADELE ADKINS
and RYAN TEDDER

ROLLING IN THE DEEP

Horn

Words and Music by ADELE ADKINS
and PAUL EPWORTH

RUMOUR HAS IT

Horn

Words and Music by ADELE ADKINS
and RYAN TEDDER

SET FIRE TO THE RAIN

HORN

Words and Music by ADELE ADKINS
and FRASER SMITH

SOMEONE LIKE YOU

Horn

Words and Music by ADELE ADKINS
and DAN WILSON

SKYFALL

from the Motion Picture SKYFALL

HORN

Words and Music by ADELE ADKINS
and PAUL EPWORTH

Slowly, with feeling

WHEN WE WERE YOUNG

Horn

Words and Music by ADELE ADKINS
and TOBIAS JESSO JR.